FUN TIMES DURING THE SEASONS
By Helen Dillon

Illustrations by Alicia Madden

Winter Fun

Fall Fun

Summer Fun

Spring Fun

To my deceased husband, Leo, my four children, Elaine, Patty, Joan, and Mark, and my two grandchildren, Jillian and Gianni.

FUN TIMES DURING THE SEASONS
By Helen Dillon

Illustrations by Alicia Madden
Edited by Marena McPherson
Designed by Lesley Etherly

ISBN-13: 978-1540602022
ISBN-10: 1540602028
Registed Copyright: TXu002004298

Playing Fall Activities

Fun Times During the Fall Season

A parade of autumn colors of red, orange, and yellow
Covered the leaves of trees
Small piles of fall leaves decorate the sidewalk.
In the distance, you can hear the strumming of a guitar
Tapping out a loud, musical tap, tap, tap.
The children respond with their feet a tap, tap, tap.
And they call their dance the Turkey Trot.

From the garden, a visit to the pumpkin patch
to choose the annual pumpkin for carving.

Pumpkins sitting on the garden wall.
Leaves on the trees have changed to
Beautiful colors of yellow, orange, red.
A song sung by the pumpkins sitting on a wall:

A pumpkin face on Halloween,
The funniest face I've ever seen.
Smiling all to see,
Girls and boys, please look at me.
With a tip of my hat and a "How do you do?"
I've a face that's very new.
Eyes cut round and nose cut square,
Smiling mouth and teeth that scare,
This hollow head is filled with space,
Oh, 'tis fun to be a pumpkin face!

Halloween Pumpkin Faces

Thanksgiving with Family

Doorbells ringing, guests arriving
For the annual Thanksgiving dinner.
Among the noise were shouts of good wishes,
Laughter, hellos, hugs, and kisses.
The family has arrived.
Drinking and toasting follows.
The toast was granted to the head of the family.
And also a toast to the cooks and the servers.

The turkey arrives displayed in an elegant manner,
Followed by hot plates of steaming vegetables,
With mouth watering food delights.
Then the family's graces,
Prepared and recited by the father of the house,
And all the guests who wished to offer a special thanks to God
For His gifts to the family.

Each person could contribute to their special thanks.
A special time was set aside for the children,
To individually give their thanks for gifts
Received during the year.
Parents were especially pleased to hear that
The children's thanks included them.

The annual Thanksgiving dinner was completed,
With many desserts, all to the delight of the guests.
All agreed this was a special Thanksgiving dinner.
Looking forward to the next Thanksgiving.
Amen!

Sledding Fun

Fun Times During the Winter Season

Outdoor ponds filled with ice.

Smooth patches for ice skating with new ice skates.

Hills covered with fresh snow

For sledding down the steep hills,

With loud screams of faster, faster, little sleigh!

Fingers tingle in the frosty air.

Wrapped up with soft, warm, wool mittens,

Scarves around the neck to say "no, no, to Mr. Cold!"

Claiming your favorite seats

Next to the open fireplace,

To watch the sparks of the fire dance

In the open flames.

To listen to the crackle of small pieces of wood

As they burn out in the last of the night.

From the front window calls Mr. Moon
Who will soon be traveling around the sky.
"Who will you meet this night on your journey?
Tell us your stories as you travel around!
Tell us about Christmas and Santa and
hearts filled with hope.
And your friends and the stars and
planets above."

In our front yard the deep snow
Invites us to build a snowman.
All the neighborhood children
Come to our yard to roll the first ball.
It is snowman's head.
Next, the second ball is rolled,
It is the body of Mr. Snowman.
And lastly, the third ball is rolled in place
As the base of our snowman.

Next, we look in Mother's sewing box
For two big black eyes,
And a piece of red material for his mouth.
We set the red cloth on his face to shape his mouth.
Buttons for eyes, a colored one for his nose,
And a strip of red material
That can be shaped as his mouth.
Good! He has a new face.

All the children in the yard are asked
To hold hands and circle the snowman,
And sing a little song:

Thank you, Mr. Snowman
Thank you, thank you, Mr. Snowman,
Thank you for coming to see me today,
To tell a story and play a game,
Before you melt away.

Thanks for pieces of chocolate candy,
I like the candy canes too,
Don't go away so fast!
I want to go with you.

Mr. Snowman Comes Alive to Play Games

Fun Times During the Spring Season

I like to feel the warmth of sunshine.

Goodbye to cold wind and snowflakes.

Green grass is everywhere,

Yellow dandelions will be popping up,

And pink tulips will show their delicate lacy insides.

Spring, sweet spring.

A sleepy robin wakes up from her nap,

And looks for other spring robins coming down the road.

She dusts her nest

With soft feathers to protect her eggs.

Down the walk, children are at play.

A section of concrete where children

With white chalk

Draw faces of their friends to amuse others walking by.

The calls of baseball, boys shouting,
"You're out!"
"You're safe!"
The baseball then flies overhead
And hits the back wall.

It's baseball time and spring.

Then to take a short walk,
To where they are selling cold pop,
Sit on the stones, drink pop, and watch people go by.

A group of girls with a jump rope doing a
Spring exercise that sounds like this:
One, Two, buckle my shoe,
Three, Four, shut the door,
Five, Six, pick up sticks,
Seven, Eight, lay them straight,
Nine, Ten, listen to the singing hen.

A Summer Nap

Fun Times During the Summer Season

Summertime is for splashing in a pool nearby,
Looking for some fresh soft sand piles,
To build a city, shape it with people, and a dog.

Resting for a nap on a soft blanket below.
Blue skies and puffy white clouds moving in the sky.
In the park, boys climbing the low limbs of young trees
To swing from limb to limb.

Searching for Strawberries

Summertime means calls to look for new strawberry patches.

Strawberries like to grow on the slanted road near the woods.

A call to my dog, Rex, tells him he is needed,

Rex keeps barking and jumping on the side hill.

There is the hint that we are close to a new patch.

Rex begins to paw the ground and there it is!

Once a year, in the small town of De Pere in Wisconsin.

The circus comes to town.

It gives thrills to the townspeople,

Who greet them with clapping and shouts of joy on their arrival.

There is the merry-go-round, the Ferris wheel,

children's games, and running races.

There are trucks selling hot dogs,

And stands that offer big ice cream cones and bars.

Come to the Circus

We sit at a table all afternoon.

Sip lemonade as a summer treat.

The high school bands from the local high schools

Provide the music, songs to sing along with.

Simply tap your feet.

All is enjoyable for the senior citizens

Who enjoy an outing.

They have fun too!

Clowns provide their own entertainment

By jumping through hoops.

They do magical tricks to make the children laugh.

And the animals do tricks.

We all sing the Merry-Go-Round song:

The Merry-Go-Round Song

A Merry-Go-Round has come to town.

My favorite you see.

Round and round,

And up and down,

My horsy carries me.

You are up.

And I am down.

As round the circle we fly.

And when the circle fades away,

We hear the children sigh.

Fall Fun

Winter Fun

Spring Fun

Summer Fun

ABOUT THE AUTHOR

Helen Dillon loved teaching and telling stories to her kindergarten, first, and third grade classes for 45 years. She is a native of Illinois, graduated from DePaul University, and has taught at Clissold, Drew, and Curtis Elementary Schools. Helen met her husband, Leo, at Curtis. Together they forged a work partnership with the sole purpose of helping children enjoy learning—Helen as a teacher and Leo as a principal. They had four children, three girls and a boy, and traveled all over the world together. They were also active in their church, St. Linus, in Oak Lawn, Illinois.

Helen was awarded "Teacher of the Year" in 1960, early in her career, by the State of Illinois. She authored four additional books: Record School, reading and math exercises which was used for research for Leo Dillon's Ph.D. dissertation, The Journey: The Rice, Summers-Dillon Family (1814-2003), Animal School House, and Dream Jobs When I Grow Up.

Helen was able to grasp what children needed to learn and created stories, poems, exercises, and inventions to make learning fun. She invented two activity stuffed bears, Charlie Countdown and Alphie Alphabet Doll, which were ultimately adapted by Mattel Toys.

In 2012, Helen's husband, Leo, passed away and she became devoted to her legacy of sharing these stories, poems, and exercises with her family and to other children. She is dedicating this book to him and to her children and grandchildren.

www.ingramcontent.com/pod-product-compliance
Lightning Source LLC
Chambersburg PA
CBHW060816290526

45792CB00005BB/1673